THE ÀJE SPIRITS

THE SACRED MOTHERS OF AIR, FIRE, WATER & EARTH

CARLOS ANTONIO DE BOURBON-GALDIANO-MONTENEGRO

AMERICAN CANDOMBLE CHURCH PUBLICATIONS, LOS ANGELES, CALIFORNIA

THE ÀJE SPIRITS

THE SACRED MOTHERS OF AIR, FIRE, WATER & EARTH

AMERICAN CANDOMBLE CHURCH PUBLICATIONS

P.O. BOX 881377

LOS ANGELES, CALIFORNIA 90009

TABLE OF CONTENTS

THE AJE SPIRITS

In modern times, the Aje Spirits have also been known to be associated with the Charites, known in Greek mythology as The Three Graces, Goddesses of such things as charm, beauty, and creativity. In Roman mythology they were known as the Gratiae.

WHAT IS SPIRITUALITY?

Spirituality can refer to an ultimate or an alleged immaterial reality; an inner path enabling a person to discover the essence of his/her being; or the "deepest values and meanings by which people live." Spiritual practices, including meditation, prayer and contemplation, are intended to develop an individual's inner life; spiritual experience includes that of connectedness with a larger reality, yielding a more comprehensive self; with other individuals or the human community; with nature or the cosmos; or with the divine realm. Spirituality is often experienced as a source of inspiration or orientation in life. It can encompass belief in immaterial realities or experiences of the immanent or transcendent nature of the world.

Traditionally, many religions have regarded spirituality as an integral aspect of religious experience.

"Spirituality exists wherever we struggle with the issues of how our lives fit into the greater scheme of things. This is true when our questions never give way to specific answers or give rise to specific practices such as prayer or meditation. We encounter spiritual issues every time we wonder where the universe comes from, why we are here, or what happens when we die. We also become spiritual when we become moved by values such as beauty, love, or creativity that seem to reveal a meaning or power beyond our visible world. An idea or practice is "spiritual" when it reveals our personal desire to establish a felt-relationship with the deepest meanings or powers governing life."

WHAT IS METAPHYSICS?

Metaphysics is a branch of philosophy concerned with explaining the fundamental nature of being and the world, although the term is not easily defined. Traditionally, metaphysics attempts to answer two basic questions in the broadest possible terms:

1."*What is there?*"

2."*What is it like?*"

A person who studies metaphysics is called a metaphysicist or a metaphysician. The metaphysician attempts to clarify the fundamental notions by which people understand the world, e.g., existence, objects and their properties, space and time, cause and effect, and possibility. A central branch of metaphysics is ontology, the investigation into the basic categories of being and how they relate to each other. Another central branch of metaphysics is cosmology, the study of the totality of all phenomena within the universe.

Prior to the modern history of science, scientific questions were addressed as a part of metaphysics known as natural philosophy. The term science itself meant "knowledge" of, originating from epistemology. The scientific method, however, transformed natural philosophy into an empirical activity deriving from experiment unlike the rest of philosophy. By the end of the 18th century, it had begun to be called "science" to distinguish it from philosophy. Thereafter, metaphysics denoted philosophical enquiry of a non-empirical character into the nature of existence. The word "metaphysics" derives from the Greek words μετά (metá) ("beyond", "upon" or "after") and φυσικά (physiká) ("physics"). It was first used as the title for several of Aristotle's works, because they were usually anthologized after the works on physics in complete editions. The prefix meta- ("beyond") indicates that these works come "after" the chapters on physics. However, Aristotle himself did not call the subject of these books "Metaphysics": he referred to it as "first philosophy." The editor of Aristotle's works, Andronicus of Rhodes, is thought to have placed the books on first philosophy right after another work, Physics, and called them τὰ μετὰ τὰ φυσικὰ βιβλία (ta meta ta physika biblia) or "the books that come after the books on physics". This was misread by Latin scholiasts, who thought it meant "the science of what is beyond the physical". However, once the name was given, the commentators sought to find intrinsic reasons for its appropriateness. For instance, it was understood to mean "the science of the world beyond nature (phusis in Greek)," that is, the science of the immaterial. Again, it was understood to refer to the chronological or pedagogical order among our philosophical studies, so that the "metaphysical sciences would mean, those that we study after having mastered the sciences that deal with the physical world". There is a widespread use of the term in current popular literature, which replicates this error, i.e. that metaphysical means spiritual non-physical: thus, "metaphysical healing" means healing by means of remedies that are not physical. The following book contains information about the Spirits of the Fourth Greater Quimbanda Kingdom of the Afro-Brazilian religious tradition known as Quimbanda. These very powerful spiritual entities are more commonly known as the Aje Spirits.

THE SACRED INITIATION MYSTERIES OF QUIMBANDA

The Afro-Brazilian religion of Quimbanda is a "mystery religion" or "gnostic religious tradition". A mystery religion is any religion with an arcanum, or secret wisdom. In a mystery religion, an inner core of beliefs, practices, and the religion's true nature, are revealed only to those who have been initiated into its secrets. An individual who desires to become a formal member of a Quimbanda temple must first petition it. If the Quimbanda spirits and the religious hierarchy accept the petition then the individual will be introduced into the mysteries through a series of initiatory rites. Acceptance within a traditional Quimbanda temple is a privilege; not a right. An initiation creates a strong emotional bond and tie between temple members, and so an initiation request should not be considered lightly by either the aspirant or the temple; and, as always, the Tata Nkisi Malongo / Yaya Nkisi Malongo has the final word. However, because of the deep bond initiation creates between the temple brothers and sisters, tradition dictates that the decision to accept a new person into the traditional Quimbanda temple must be unanimous. If only one person in the temple, can state good reason, and cannot be persuaded otherwise by other temple initiates, then entrance is denied to the Initiate. Again, the Tata Nkisi Malongo / Yaya Nkisi Malongo has the final word in all things temple related. In the Quimbanda religious tradition, initiation is considered a "rite of passage". In the context of ritual magic and esotericism, an initiation is considered to cause a fundamental process of change to begin within the person being initiated. There are various initiations associated with the Quimbanda religious tradition. In a traditional Quimbanda Temple it will take seven years to complete all of the sacred initiation in order to be called, Tata Nkisi Malongo (Male) or Yaya Nkisi Malongo (Woman). The various steps of initiation are called degrees. Each degree is a step in that initiation process. There are seven degrees of initiation in the Quimbanda religious tradition at the American Candomble Church. These seven degrees are known as the "Seven Greater Quimbanda Mysteries". There are also many other initiations associated with the "Seven Greater Quimbanda Mysteries" of the Quimbanda religious tradition, but these are considered minor initiations. These minor initiation rituals are called the "Lesser Quimbanda Mysteries". The minor initiation rituals are found within the confines of the "Seven Greater Quimbanda Mysteries". All initiation rituals are done at the temple or in nature. A Quimbanda temple is a place of worship and where initiated individuals come together as a "family unit" to venerate the vast pantheon of Quimbanda deities and spirits. These initiation rituals can take various years to complete. An individual who is not initiated into the Afro-Brazilian Congo mysteries can spiritually initiate themselves or spiritually align themselves with the powerful force of the Aje spiritual realm.

INTRODUCTION TO THE AJE SPIRITS

The Aje Spirits are invisible spiritual entities that coexists with humans here on Earth. It is believed that the Aje Spirits are powerful "Witches" that control all aspects of human destiny including such things as happiness, wealth, love, health and personal relationships. It is also believed that if an individual does not make a spiritual peace and truce with the powerful Aje Spirits that they can cause great harm and bring about great tragedy to all human beings. The Aje Spirits were here even before the first man and first woman appeared on this Earth. Since the time that man and woman first appeared here on Earth, the Aje Spirits have been in spiritual competition with humans and historically have many of times tried to eliminate all life of mankind through such negative acts as causing famines, disease and even natural catastrophes and disasters such as floods and earthquakes. By receiving the blessings of these powerful spiritual entities you will be establishing a personal relationship with them so they will not cause you any personal harm or misfortune. For all of these reasons just mentioned, that is why it is very important to receive their Mysteries. If the Aje Spirits are not ritually appeased then an individual will never be able to fully accomplish their spiritual goals associated with their birth destiny. Although the traditional Aje Spirits Initiation Ceremony takes 21 days to complete the ritual initiation ceremony, this book will instruct how to spiritually initiate yourself or spiritually align yourself with the powerful force of the Aje spiritual realm.

The powerful Aje Spirits can be petitioned in all matters of spiritual protection, spell casting, attracting love, wealth, court success and to overcome any and all difficult obstacles in your path.

The Mother of the Aje Spirits is named *Iyami Osoronga*.

The Aje Spirits are identified with the famous Greek statue of the "Three Graces" or in religious picture form as the "Three Sisters," "Faith, Hope & Charity". There are several initiation formulas and ways to present the Aje Spirits, but the following is one of the most powerful and effective manners for individuals to spiritually align themselves with this powerful elemental force without going through any type of formal initiation. By following the initiation formula below you will see spectacular magical results.

Normally, there are (5) sacred items that must be prepared in order to successfully give this initiation to an individual. Together all (5) sacred items are collectively called the "AJE SPIRITS". It is through these (5) very important religious items that the powerful Aje Spirits will be able to assist you when you summon them to our dimension from where they dwell. If you do not have all of the following sacred religious items at your shrine for the "Aje Spirits" they will not be able to manifest to you when summoning them. These (5) sacred religious items are the sacred "*OKOBELEFO*"(Clay Ceramic pot that will be housing the Mysteries of the Aje Spirits / Aje Spirits Nganga)", "*ORERE*" (Ozun De Aje)", "*TITILLERO*", (Hollow Gourd/Calabash), "*MPAKA*" and the "*MBELE*" (Machete). For those individuals who are not formally initiated into the mysteries of Afro-Brazilian Quimbanda, you will not have access to receive these items so everything must be done spiritually. Many people believe to receive the spiritual mysteries of the Aje is more powerful than to actually receive the actual religious items in a traditional initiation ritual.

The following initiation ceremony of how to present the Mysteries of the Aje Spirits is taken from the Afro-Brazilian Congo tradition known as Quimbanda and as practiced in my Brazilian Orthodox Quimbanda Congo Munanzo. Although there are many initiation methods and variations of how to correctly present the Aje Spirits, if you follow this presented method you will witness and experience the spiritual power of the Aje Spirits in all of their "Splendor and Glory".

Once you have received the Aje Spirits Mysteries you will see your life start to change immediately overnight into success. All of your everyday problems will completely vanish.

HOW TO PRESENT THE AJE SPIRITS INITIATION CEREMONY

The Aje Spirits Initiation Ceremony is one of the most beautiful ceremonies of the Congo religion. When an individual receives this initiation the "Divine Universal Forces" are called to descend down upon the ritual to bestow to the new initiate the "spiritual right" to walk in the invisible world of the Aje Spirits with authority and command. This sacred ceremony links the new initiate to the invisible world of the powerful Aje Spirits who are the rightful owners of and who govern the Universal Laws of the (4) Elements of Earth. These (4) Elements are Air, Water, Earth and Fire. When the new initiate receives this initiation they will be given the authority of how to use the "secret keys of knowledge" to be able to spiritually work with these (4) Universal Elements which are necessary and are involved in all spiritual or magical manifestations. All (4) Universal Elements are considered and believed to be "Universal Elements of Creation." Therefore in your magical work of reality creation, these (4) Universal Elements must be used for your magical manifestations to be complete. The reason for any failure of magical manifestation is only because of misalignment in any of these (4) Universal Elements. The number (4) is the "number of creation." The more you know about the universe, the better you can create powerful magic.

The first Universal Element which is governed by the Aje Spirits is Air. This element represents intention. Wind or air is the mental plane of reality. It is the plane of pure information or data. In using the Universal Element of wind, you are dealing with pure thought. In this realm, you can use visualization, affirmation and pure intent which can also be referred to as goal setting. These three activities take place on the mental plane. You can use any of these three or all of them together. Have an intent or goal to achieve, visualize the outcome and affirm that it is materialized.

The second Universal Element which is governed by the Aje Spirits is Water. This element represents emotion. Water is the emotional or astral plane of reality. It is the plane of desire. Whatever you feel manifests first on this plane. In this realm, you can use the act of generating emotion for manifestation. This is where you get the feeling of having already attained your desire. Energy is needed for creation and your feeling is the energy. Feelings of peace, joy and gratitude provides the energy for manifesting like conditions. Your feeling is resonance and attraction.

The third Universal Element which is governed by the Aje Spirits is Earth. This element represents action. Earth is the ethereal and physical plane of reality. It is the plane of materialization. Many a times, your desires already exist in the mental and emotional plane of reality, but you are required to take action to complete the manifestation process. Inspired action is the avenue by which ideas are brought into form on the material plane. Action is what enables you to be part of the manifestation process. The joy is in experiencing creation happening through you.

The forth Universal Element which is governed by the Aje Spirits is Fire. This element represents righteousness. Fire is the soul or causal plane of reality. It is the plane of divine will. If your intentions are in alignment with the intents of your higher self, then it has allowance to manifest. You may have visualized, felt your desire as a reality and taken inspired action but still haven't experienced the manifestation of your desire. That is because according to righteousness, it is not the right time or setting. Your higher self is handling the entire process of unfoldment.

Although there are four Universal Elements of creation, there is also a fifth one by which all four elemental mysteries arise from. The fifth Universal Element is emptiness or void. It is not really empty or void but it is simply pure, undefined energy. This energy is consciousness which is differentiated into all four aspects of itself which are intent, emotion, action and higher intent. One must bring the mind to a state of emptiness by clearing all thoughts except for one, which is the intent. From a state of single mindedness, your intention has great clarity.

All four Universal Elements of your magical desires and or manifestation must be working in harmony with one another for it to succeed. You must visualize and affirm what you desire instead of what you do not desire. You must feel the joy of having your desire instead of the fear of lacking it. You must do everything in alignment with your intent instead of acting in ways that are opposite to it. You must also detach and trust in divine order and divine timing of your higher self to arrange the unfoldment. With the four Universal Elements in spiritual alignment with the Aje Spirits, you cannot fail.

There is also another aspect of righteousness which is karma. Virtuous deeds will be recompensed by desirable gains while deeds that lack virtue will attract retribution. The great Universe is a mirror. What you do will be reflected back to you. Give and it shall be given back to you. When you express abundance by giving to others for their gain, the

Universe will reflect your virtuous deeds with greater abundance. Your desires have more power to manifest when you have generated a store of good karma for yourself. Within righteousness is also your sense of deserving. If you want something but do not believe that you deserve to have it, your conflicting belief will repel your desire away from you. If you want to receive what you desire, you must believe that you have the right to have it. The why behind your intention is also your fire to achieve it. When you have a purpose for achieving something, you will be driven towards it. Fire is what supplements your thoughts, emotions and actions with the energy to keep on persisting. The purpose behind an intent also determines its power to manifest. When you desire something for the greatest good of yourself and the universe, your intention is highly imbued with virtue. Any intent that is directly aligned with the nature of the universal mind will be aided by the entire Universe itself. That is because you are not just having a personal intent but you are taking on the intents of the Universe. Intents that are love based come from a holistic point of view. If Nzambi (God) is for you, who can be against you? When something isn't happening for you, use wisdom to consider what might be a better intention to have? The Universe is always working everything for your highest good, and it is always giving you what you really want. The Universe is your total self and therefore you are never denied your true will. Your magical manifestations can also happen faster and more easily when you have opportunities and contacts set up on the physical plane. Success sets the stage for further success. Everything plays a part in Universal Spiritual completion. Without a new initiate undergoing this very important initiation by which you make a pact with the Aje Spirits and establish a peaceful relationship with these powerful entities you will not be able to accomplish any magical goals. If a new initiate does not undergo a ritual with the Aje Spirits which binds us to their world the Congo magician will find it almost impossible to achieve their magical desires with accuracy. Because these powerful entities are naturally found within nature, the Aje Spirits Initiation Ceremony usually is done outdoors and in open nature. The best time to receive this initiation would be on a "New Moon" or a "Full Moon". The initiation can be done during the daylight hours.

If you receive this initiation and make a spiritual pact "spiritual truce" with them nothing that you do magically will be impossible. If a new initiate does not undergo this initiation with the Aje Spirits you will be always be plagued with the perils of life. These powerful Aje Spirits which are more than often times overlooked because out of fear or ignorance by initiates of Congo religion must be appeased first in order to be able to gain control and spiritual command within the invisible spiritual world.

PART I

The first part of this initiation begins with a ritual bath. You must be spiritually clean to receive any mysteries of the Afro-Brazilian Quimbanda religious tradition. You can use traditional African Black Soap known as Dudu-Osun. These soaps are available from most African general stores and companies that sell occult supplies.

Before doing the actual Aje Spiritual Dedication ceremony, the individual must prepare three days before by fasting. Fasting for the purpose of this book means limited food portions at each meal to cleanse the body, mind and soul.

The individual will also meditate on the mysteries of the Aje Spirits (the four Elemental Mysteries) and a genuine spiritual self-reflection about the importance of the spiritual commitment which you will be entering into with the spiritual world of the Aje Spirits and the Afro-Brazilian Quimbanda religious tradition.

After three days of spiritual fasting then do the following ritual. This ritual can be started at any given hour after you take your daily shower using the African Black Soap.

If you are not able to find and purchase the African Black Soap then just proceed with the ritual without it. Either way, you must bathe before doing any major initiation ritual associated with the Quimbanda religious tradition. If you would like to have a pair of Aje Spirit beads, you can order a set of consecrated beads from the American Candomble

Church. The beads can be used for spiritual protection and good fortune.

PART II

After taking your ritual bath, find a quiet location where you can quietly meditate on the mysteries of the Aje Spirits and recite the following initiation prayers.

PART III

Standing towards the East, do and say the following:

NEW INITIATE:

With the blessings of Nzambi, the God of Heaven and Earth, Sala Malekun, Malekun Sala - Sarava

With the blessings of Exu Maioral, the Guardian of the First Greater Quimbanda Kingdom - Sala Malekun, Malekun Sala - Sarava

With the blessings of Exu Rei, the Guardian of the Second Greater Quimbanda Kingdom - Sala Malekun, Malekun Sala - Sarava

With the blessings of Maria Padilla Reina, the Guardian of the Third Greater Quimbanda Kingdom - Sala Malekun, Malekun Sala - Sarava

With the blessings of Aje Spirits, the Guardians of the Fourth Greater Quimbanda Kingdom - Sala Malekun, Malekun Sala - Sarava

With the blessings of my ancestors, my spirit guides that walk with me, the Preto Velhos, the Guardians of the Fifth Greater Quimbanda Kingdom - Sala Malekun, Malekun Sala - Sarava

With the blessings of spirits of the Congo, the Guardians of the Sixth Greater Quimbanda Kingdom - Sala Malekun, Malekun Sala - Sarava

With the blessings of Caboclos, the Guardians of the Seventh Greater Quimbanda Kingdom - Sala Malekun, Malekun Sala - Sarava

With the blessings of the sacred Guardians of the Seven Lesser Quimbanda Kingdoms - Sala Malekun, Malekun Sala - Sarava

On this most sacred of all days, I (say your name), do summon the Aje Spirits from their realm to witness this sacred ceremony. Sala Malekun, Malekun Sala - Sarava

NEW INITIATE:

Standing towards the East, do and say the following:

Using your right hand, make the sign of the Quimbanda Trinity Cross over your body. The Quimbanda Trinity sign of the Cross is made by touching the hand sequentially to the forehead, lower chest or navel area, and right shoulder,then left shoulder and then placing your hands together in a praying position and then kissing your right hand three times.

This is how to say and do this: at the forehead, *IN THE NAME OF NZAMBI*; at the naval, *IN THE NAME OF EXU MAIORAL*; across to the right shoulder, *IN THE NAME OF EXU REI*; across to the right left shoulder, *IN THE NAME OF MARIA PADILLA REINA*; and finally to the center of your heart while placing your hands together in a praying position, *SARAVA*; afterwards kiss your hands three times.

NEW INITIATE:

BEFORE ME STANDS THE ARCHANGEL RAPHAEL. BEHIND ME STANDS THE ARCHANGEL GABRIEL. ON MY RIGHT HAND, THE ARCHANGEL MICHAEL AND ON MY LEFT HAND THE ARCHANGEL AURIEL.

NEW INITIATE:

Standing towards the West, do and say the following:

Using your right hand, make the sign of the Quimbanda Trinity Cross over your body. The Quimbanda Trinity sign of the Cross is made by touching the hand sequentially to the forehead, lower chest or navel area, and right shoulder, then left shoulder and then placing your hands together in a praying position and then kissing your right hand three times. This is how to say and do this: at the forehead, *IN THE NAME OF NZAMBI*; at the naval, *IN THE NAME OF EXU MAIORAL*; across to the right shoulder, *IN THE NAME OF EXU REI*; across to the right left shoulder, *IN THE NAME OF MARIA PADILLA REINA*; and finally to the center of your heart while placing your hands together in a praying position, *SARAVA*; afterwards kiss your hands three times.

NEW INITIATE:

Standing towards the South, do and say the following:

Using your right hand, make the sign of the Quimbanda Trinity Cross over your body. The Quimbanda Trinity sign of the Cross is made by touching the hand sequentially to the forehead, lower chest or navel area, and right shoulder, then left shoulder and then placing your hands together in a praying position and then kissing your right hand three times. This is how to say and do this: at the forehead, *IN THE NAME OF NZAMBI*; at the naval, *IN THE NAME OF EXU MAIORAL*; across to the right shoulder, *IN THE NAME OF EXU REI*; across to the right left shoulder, *IN THE NAMF OF MARIA PADILLA REINA*; and finally to the center of your heart while placing your hands together in a praying position, *SARAVA*; afterwards kiss your hands three times.

NEW INITIATE:

Standing towards the North, do and say the following:

Using your right hand, make the sign of the Quimbanda Trinity Cross over your body. The Quimbanda Trinity sign of the Cross is made by touching the hand sequentially to the forehead, lower chest or navel area, and right shoulder, then left shoulder and then placing your hands together in a praying position and then kissing your right hand three times. This is how to say and do this: at the forehead, *IN THE NAME*

OF NZAMBI; at the naval, *IN THE NAME OF EXU MAIORAL*; across to the right shoulder, *IN THE NAME OF EXU REI*; across to the right left shoulder, *IN THE NAME OF MARIA PADILLA REINA*; and finally to the center of your heart while placing your hands together in a praying position, *SARAVA*; afterwards kiss your hands three times.

NEW INITIATE:

Standing towards the East, do and say the following:

FOR AROUND MY BODY PROTECTED BY THE DIVINE LIGHT OF THE FLAMES OF THE QUIMBANDA TRINITY - Sala Malekun, Malekun Sala - Sarava

IN THE NAME OF NZAMBI, THE GOD OF THE HEAVENS AND THE EARTH - Sala Malekun, Malekun Sala - Sarava

IN THE NAME OF EXU MAIORAL - Sala Malekun, Malekun Sala - Sarava

IN THE NAME OF EXU REI - Sala Malekun, Malekun Sala - Sarava

IN THE NAME OF MARIA PADILLA REINA - Sala Malekun, Malekun Sala - Sarava

IN THE NAME OF THE QUIMBANDA TRINITY - Sala Malekun, Malekun Sala - Sarava

I, say you're your complete birth name, INVOKE THE SACRED AND DIVINE POWERS OF THE QUIMBANDA TRINITY IN THE NAME NZAMBI - Sala Malekun, Malekun Sala - Sarava

I, say your complete birth name, TODAY ON THIS MOST SACRED OF ALL DAYS COME NOW BEFORE NZAMBI AND THE QUIMBANDA TRINITY, WITH COMPLETE UNDERSTANDING OF THE QUIMBANDA RELIGIOUS TRADITION AND COMPLETELY ON MY OWN FREE WILL - Sala Malekun, Malekun Sala - Sarava

The New Initiate does and says the following:

Using your right hand, tap your center of your chest directly over your heart three times and then the following;

I, say your complete birth name, INVOKE THE DIETIES AND SPIRITS OF THE QUIMBANDA RELIGIOUS TRADITION TO GRANT ME ACCESS INTO THE MYSTERIES OF THE AJE SPIRITS. I KNOCK AT YOUR SACRED DOOR TO THE HEAVENLY REALM TO OPEN UP THE GATES OF THE SEVEN QUIMBANDA KINGDOMS. - Sala Malekun, Malekun Sala - Sarava

WITH THE BLESSINGS OF THE KINGDOM OF KING, EXU MAIORAL, THE SEVEN MOST HOLY ARCHANGELS THAT WATCH OVER THE ASTRAL REALM AND COMMAND THE 72 SPIRITS OF EXU - Sala Malekun, Malekun Sala - Sarava

WITH THE BLESSINGS OF THE KINGDOM OF KING, EXU REI, GUARDIAN OF THE MYSTERIES OF THE CROSSROADS, GUARDIAN OF HUMAN FATE, DESTINY AND THE DELIVERER OF THE SACRED DIVINE WORD. DIVINE EMPEROR TO THE SECRETS OF THE CELESTIAL CONSTELLATIONS - Sala Malekun, Malekun Sala - Sarava

WITH THE BLESSINGS OF THE KINGDOM OF QUEEN, MARIA PADILLA REINA, GUARDIAN OF THE MYSTERIES AND PLEASURES OF LIFE, DIVINE EMPRESS TO THE SECRETS OF THE

SEVEN PLANETS - HEAR ME NOW O MIGHTY QUEEN OF THE CROSSROADS - Sala Malekun, Malekun Sala - Sarava

WITH THE BLESSINGS OF THE KINGDOM OF THE AJE SPIRITS, THE DIVINE INVISIBLE MOTHERS OF THE SACRED MARKETPLACE, THE WEAVERS OF TIME AND OF THE ELEMENTAL MYSTERIES - Sala Malekun, Malekun Sala - Sarava

WITH THE BLESSINGS OF MY ANCESTORS WHO ARE KNEELING AT THE FOOT OF NZAMBI IN LIGHT. WITH THE BLESSINGS OF THE PRETO VELHOS AND OF THE SPIRIT GUIDES - Sala Malekun, Malekun Sala - Sarava

WITH THE BLESSINGS OF THE KINGDOM OF THE QUIMBANDA CONGO SPIRITS (NKISI) - Sala Malekun, Malekun Sala - Sarava

WITH THE BLESSINGS OF THE KINGDOM OF THE MOST SACRED AND DIVINE SPIRITS OF THE CABOCLOS - Sala Malekun, Malekun Sala - Sarava

I, say your complete birth name, INVOKE THE SACRED AND DIVINE POWERS OF THE AJE SPIRITS IN THE NAME NZAMBI - Sala Malekun, Malekun Sala - Sarava

NEW INITIATE:

I (SAY YOUR NAME), invoke the powers of the Aje Spirits, the Mothers of the Sacred Marketplace,

The Mothers of Invisibility, The Mothers of the (4) Universal Elemental Forces (Earth, Water, Fire and Air). - Sala Malekun, Malekun Sala - Sarava

I have come here today on this most sacred day to call upon the Aje Spirits, The Divine Mothers of the Night to grant us the power and the connection to deliver the "Sacred Word." Cover us with your Divine Protective Light and Protect us from all Evil and deliver us from our Enemies. Our Enemies are your Enemies and Your Enemies are Our Enemies. Sala Malekun, Malekun Sala - Sarava

O Divine Mothers, Aje. I invoke you from the North, South, East and the West to hear our prayers and to come from where you live and from where you are. Sala Malekun, Malekun Sala - Sarava

I have not come here tonight to challenge you or to make war and fight with you, because we know that we would not win. Sala Malekun, Malekun Sala - Sarava

I call upon Nzambi the Creator of the Heavens and the Earth to witness this sacred ritual. Sala Malekun, Malekun Sala - Sarava

I call upon Gonda (the Congo God of the Moon) to witness this sacred ritual. Sala Malekun, Malekun Sala - Sarava

I call upon our Ancestors who are kneeling at the Foot of Nzambi (God) in Light to witness this ritual. Sala Malekun, Malekun Sala - Sarava

I call upon the Spirit Exu, the Divine Gate Keeper, to witness this ritual. Sala Malekun, Malekun Sala - Sarava

NEW INITIATE:

I call upon the Congo Spirit Ozain, the Keeper of the Mystical and Magical Secrets of the Divine Aje Spirits to witness this ritual. Sala Malekun, Malekun Sala - Sarava

I call upon the Congo Spirits to witness this ritual and to bestow their blessings to all present here and to (say the name of the new initiate) who is knocking at your divine cosmic door of sacred knowledge. Sala Malekun, Malekun Sala - Sarava

NEW INITIATE:

DIVINE MOTHERS, AJE, BESTOW YOUR POWERS UPON ME.

AJE BRILLUMBI NDOKI INFIERNO VIRA MUNDO

AJE BRILLUMBI NDOKI INFIERNO VIRA MUNDO

AJE BRILLUMBI NDOKI INFIERNO VIRA MUNDO

AJE BRILLUMBI NDOKI INFIERNO VIRA MUNDO

AJE BRILLUMBI NDOKI INFIERNO VIRA MUNDO

AJE BRILLUMBI NDOKI INFIERNO VIRA MUNDO

AJE BRILLUMBI NDOKI INFIERNO VIRA MUNDO

AJE BRILLUMBI NDOKI INFIERNO VIRA MUNDO

AJE BRILLUMBI NDOKI INFIERNO VIRA MUNDO

WHO IS THE GREATEST IN HEAVEN? NZAMBI

WHO IS THE GREATEST IN HEAVEN? NZAMBI

WHO IS THE GREATEST IN HEAVEN? NZAMBI

WHO ARE YOU? AJE

WHO ARE YOU? AJE

WHO ARE YOU? AJE

ON THIS MOST SACRED AND HOLY OF ALL DAYS, I (SAY YOUR NAME) DO INVOKE THE MYSTERIES OF THE AJE SPIRITS.

WITH THE BLESSINGS OF NZAMBI AND THE SEVEN GREATER QUIMBANDA KINGDOMS AND THE SEVEN LESSER QUIMBANDA KINGDOMS, I CAUSE THIS RITUAL INTO BEING.

SALA MALEKUN, MALEKUN SALA - SARAVA

A PICTURE OF THE AJE SPIRIT MYSTERIES AT THEIR SACRED SHRINE AT THE AMERICAN CANDOMBLE CHURCH.

THE SACRED AJE SPIRIT SHRINE AT THE AMERICAN CANDOMBLE CHURCH.

ELEMENTAL MAGIC SPELLS

Many people who practice witchcraft like to use elemental magic spells, as it is a very natural form of magic. It's also much easier to learn (and remember) the basic qualities and attributes of 4 elements rather than learn hundreds of other correspondences for herbs, stones or oils. Though it may be simpler than some other spells, elemental magic spells can still be powerful.

THE ELEMENT OF AIR

First off, we have the element of air. The qualities that air represents include: ideas, inspiration, creativity, intelligence, travel, freedom, new beginnings and mental clarity. If you want a spell for any of these ideas, you should incorporate air into your magic. Items like feathers, bells, incense and quartz all have air attributes.

THE ELEMENT OF EARTH

Next is earth. This is an element that stands for grounding, all forms of nature, money and prosperity, growth, rules and responsibility. If you want to represent earth on your altar, you can use a pentacle, stones, or a bowl of earth or rock salt. For earth spells, crystals and herbs are often used since they are natural items directly from the earth.

THE ELEMENT OF FIRE

Next up for elemental magic spells is fire. Candle spells are the most popular kind of witchcraft spell, and are a good example of using fire. Fire should be used for spells involving passion, energy, strength, creativity and anger. Items for fire include candles (obviously) as well as volcanic glass, and the athame (though some traditions have the athame associated with air). Fire spells usually involve candles, but not always.

THE ELEMENT OF WATER

And lastly we come to water. Water energies are often used in spells for love, fertility, friendship, healing and sleep. But spells don't often call for actual water. Crystals like aquamarine and moonstone make great "water" additions, as do herbs like lilac. A chalice is the usual altar tool to represent the element of water. If you do use water in your water spells, try to use naturally collected rainwater.

QUIMBANDA MAGIC & LUNAR PHASES

One complete cycle of the moon takes exactly 28 days to complete, the same average time for a woman's menstrual cycle. This is no accident. A woman's body is something of a mirror of the moon and her ways. In many ways the difference between the sun and the moon are very similar to the differences between men and women. The different personalities the moon presents throughout her cycle have perhaps the most profound effect on ritual workings than any other Time Correspondence. In order to coordinate your ritual workings with the cycles of the moon, you can follow the generalized guidelines below or the more advanced guidelines.

***Note that the more *Time Correspondences* you add to your ritual workings, the less you will need to rely on the more advanced system of the lunar cycle. And, in fact, sometimes you will be unable to use the more advanced system especially if you try to incorporate either the Lunar Zodiacal Calendar or the system of the Days of the Week. In all, familiarize yourself with all systems, but use what works best for you.

The Waxing Moon

Magic for increases that mirror the increasing size of the moon including: healings, prosperity, attraction, success, gains, love, increases, friendship, protection and any other positive magic. The horns on the crescent you see in the sky during the waxing phase of the moon are facing to your left.

The Full Moon

For the rituals that require the most potent and powerful magic, the fullest phase of the moon is most appropriate. Though there is some controversy over what kind of magic is most appropriate during the full moon, protection and any other dire situation in which a great deal of energy is needed in order to attain ritual success are universally accepted as appropriate at this time. The full moon is the point when the moon reflects all light from the sun back to the earth. It is the most potent time of the lunar cycle.

The Waning Moon

Magic for decreases that mirror the decreasing size of the moon including: banishings, exorcisms, cleansings, magic to rid yourself of a bad habit, any type of ritual to rid yourself of negativity whether it is from human or spirit sources. The horns on the crescent you see in the sky during the waning phase of the moon are facing to your right.

The Black Moon

This particular phase of the moon carries some controversy. Some practitioners insist that no magic be performed on this night, however, next to the full moon, the black moon is the second most potent time of the lunar cycle. Either highly difficult banishings that have been resistant to rituals performed on other nights of the waning moon can be abolished during this night when the moon is at its blackest in the sky. However, take care to perform these banishing before the moon is at its darkest point otherwise the moon will no longer be the Black Moon, but the New Moon which is associated with beginnings rather than endings.

The New Moon

The new phase of the moon begins when the moon is hidden from sight due to the earth's position between the sun and the moon. No sunlight is reflected back down to us from the moon's surface. This phase is sometimes mistaken for the Black Moon, which directly precedes it. The New Moon and all its accompanying characteristics can be relevant from three days after the darkest point of the moon. Experiment to determine how best this system works for you. During this time, the following types of ritual/spell work are most appropriate: As the newest and earliest point in a new moon cycle, the new moon is seen by most practitioners as the most appropriate time to begin new projects, new spells and any rituals that require many days to complete has passed into the more powerful phase, the waxing gibbous phase. With rituals that require less lunar potency or are the first in a line of several consecutive rituals that lead up to the full moon, you can confidently use this phase of the moon. For example, a healing performed to ease a cold or mild chronic illness can easily be started during the waxing crescent phase of the moon. However, a more serious illness would be better served during the waxing gibbous phase. Ideally, with some minor examples, nearly all magic would be best divided out between the full or new moon, but this is such a short period of time each month, that we delegate certain phases to certain less important tasks. However, remember two things. For very serious illnesses the full (for healing the illness) or black (for banishing the illness) moons are the best choices, but they are not always necessary for more minor problems. Also the time does come sometimes when we have no choice but to do ritual work during incompatible times. In emergency cases, don't let bad timing stop you. Use other Nature Correspondences or the other types of magic (Mental or Spiritual Magic) to offset your lack of timing.

WAXING CRESENT MOON

This period is especially favorable in all matters concerning growth, protection, healing advancement, abundance, to increase knowledge, spirituality, and fertility, new beginnings or to draw something to you.

The Waxing Half Moon

This unique time of the month allows for all forms of positive magic that can otherwise be performed on the waxing phase of the moon, however, the waxing half-moon is special in that you can perform magic during this time if you are engaged in a situation that is teetering on the edge of two resolutions and you want the result to turn out in your favor or in some positive fashion. For example if you wanted to do a spell for the success of a court case in which your lawyer predicts that you have a 50-50 chance of winning, you could do the spell on the half waxing moon to ensure that the situation will have a favorable outcome.

The Waxing Gibbous Moon

Similar to the waxing crescent phase, you can perform all actions compatible with increase during this time period. However, magic that requires more lunar energy than the waxing crescent can provide should if possible be delayed until this time period because of its closer proximity to the full moon. Of course minor magical workings can also be performed during this time as well, but the added energy here may not be absolutely necessary.

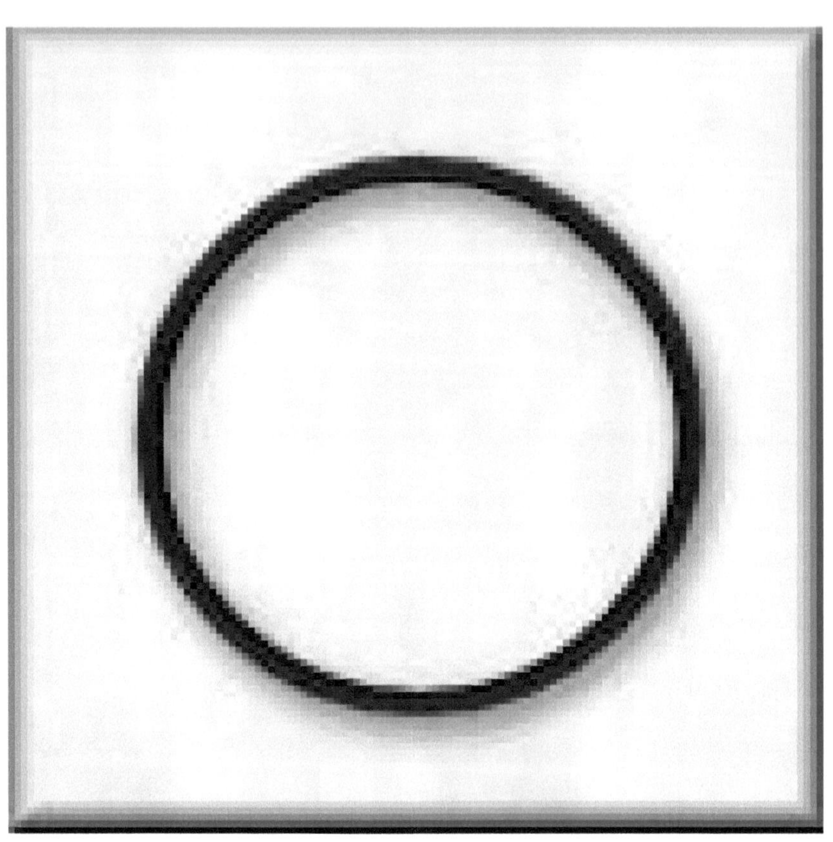

The Full Moon

The moon in its fullest phase reflects all the light sent to it by the sun. The earth is completely out of the path between these two bodies and the energy of the moon is at its most potent. The full moon is the most potent time of the entire month and the time when many traditions of witchcraft hold their Sabbaths, or ritual gatherings or celebrations. Since there is so much controversy over what actually begins and ends the cycle of the moon, there is some discrepancy over what kind of magic is best performed during this time. Technically, the full moon is the middle of the moon's cycle when the positive aspects of the moon's influence are at their peak, however many practitioners view the full moon as an down slope rather than a peak and thus either of the two types of magic below may be performed a full three days before the full moon depending on your personal preference. Many people prefer to only perform full moon rituals on the day of the full moon, but as with all other things in magic, feel free to experiment. What works for one person may not work for you and vice versa. Positive magic of any kind including completions of spells begun during the new moon or any other positive spell that requires massive lunar energy to propel a ritual intention into being. Fortunately not all spells require this much energy and some magicians consider performing trivial workings during this time as "overkill". However, you will have to decide for yourself how serious a working is to you to decide whether it warrants waiting until the full moon. Experience is the best teacher here. Negative magic as in banishings, exorcisms, cleansings or bindings. Protective magic while not necessarily negative is extremely effective when performed on the full moon.

The Waning Gibbous Moon

The relationship between the waning gibbous and waning crescent phases of the moon are opposite to those of the waxing phase because as the moon approaches the darkest point, it's decreasing potency grows. Thus as it moves from waning gibbous to half waning to waning crescent, it becomes more powerful in decreasing energies. So for minor decreasing and banishing rituals, the waning gibbous moon is more appropriate because not as much lunar decreasing energy is required to be successful. However for more serious decreases and banishings, the waning crescent moon is most appropriate because of its closer proximity to the black moon (the greatest point of decrease).

The Waning Half Moon

This is another unique time of the month which allows for all forms of banishing or decreasing magic that can otherwise be performed on the waning phase of the moon. However, the waning half-moon is special in that you can perform magic during this time if you are engaged in a situation that is teetering on the edge of two resolutions and you want the result to turn out in your favor or in some decreasing fashion. For example if you wanted to do a spell to keep yourself from being audited (in essence decreasing the problem) and you thought that you have about a 50-50 chance of this happening, then you could do the spell on the half waning moon to ensure that the threat of an audit will diminish and eventually disappear.

The Waning Crescent Moon

Rituals that require more energy for banishment though not necessarily the raw power of the black moon are best performed during this time as the waning crescent phase of the moon is close enough to the black moon that it carries a good portion of its lunar decreasing energy with it.

The Black Moon

The Black moon, also called the Dark Moon and the Lost Moon, is the point when the moon is at its darkest in the sky. It is the end of the moon cycle when the absence of light in the sky reflects a void. Therefore by this theory, the black moon is the most appropriate time to perform banishings, cleansings, exorcisms and other rejectionary forms of magic. Do your own experimentation to determine which system (or both) is right for you.

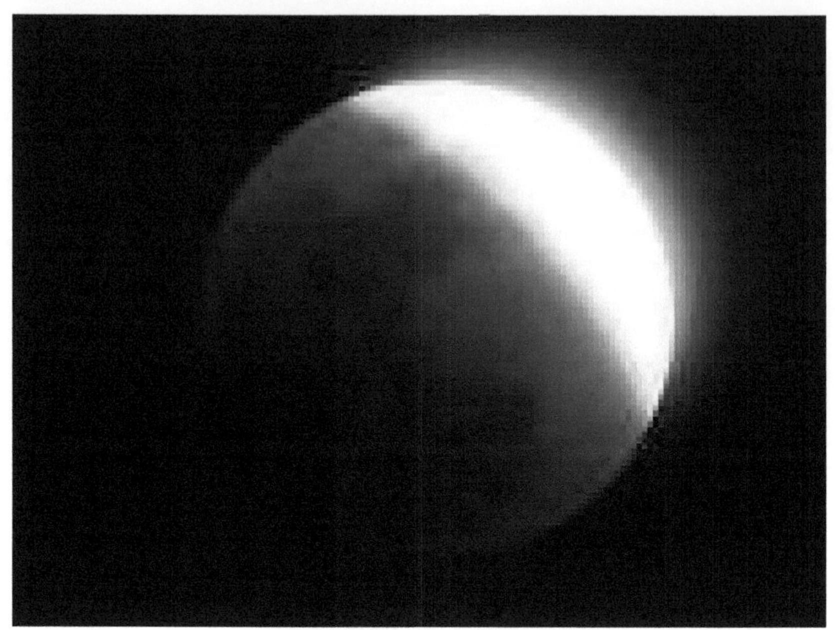

LUNAR ECLIPSE

The lunar eclipse represents the perfect union of the Sun and the Moon. Any type of magic is acceptable.

SOLAR ECLIPSE

During a Solar eclipse, it is good to do magical works of banishing negative people from your life and to banish away negative habits or negative thought process.

RITUAL TO INVOKE THE POWERS OF THE AJE SPIRITS

THIS SACRED RITUAL TO THE POWERFUL AJE SPIRITS IS USED TO REMOVE OBSTACLES IN YOUR PATH AND TO REMOVE NEGATIVE VIBRATIONS.

THE FOLLOWING RITUAL SHOULD BE DONE FOR 9 CONSECUTIVE DAYS.

STEP 1

1. Draw the spirit signature of the Aje Spirits directly on the ground / dirt using a stick or your fingers.

2. Using your right hand, make the sign of the Quimbanda Trinity Cross over your body. The Quimbanda Trinity sign of the Cross is made by touching the hand sequentially to the forehead, lower chest or navel area, and right shoulder,then left shoulder and then placing your hands together in a praying position and then kissing your right hand three times. This is how to say and do this: at the forehead, *IN THE NAME OF NZAMBI;* at the naval, *IN THE NAME OF EXU MAIORAL;* across to the right shoulder, *IN THE NAME OF EXU REI*; across to the right left shoulder, *IN THE NAME OF MARIA PADILLA REINA*; and finally to the center of your heart while placing your hands together in a praying position, *SARAVA*; afterwards kiss your hands three times.

If you have a brass bell you can use it during ritual if you are not able to have a ritual bell then just leave it out of the ritual

(FACE THE NORTH DIRECTION WHILE RINGING THE BELL AND THEN TURN TO THE SOUTH , THEN TURN TO THE EAST AND THEN TURN TO THE WEST AND THEN TURN TO FACE THE RITUAL AREA.

I CALL UPON THE GREAT FORCE OF THE UNIVERSE TO SUR-ROUND MY BODY WITH PROTECTIVE LIGHT TO MAKE ME INVISI-BLE TONIGHT SO THAT MY ENEMIES KNOWN AND UNKNOWN WILL NOT BE ABLE TO SEE NOR HEAR WHAT I AM ABOUT TO DO. I CALL UPON MY ANCESTORS WHO ARE KNEELING AT THE FOOT OF GOD IN LIGHT THAT THEY HEAR MY

REQUEST AND GRANT ME SIGHT. OZAIN SEND ME A WIND, OZAIN SEND ME A BREEZE AND SUMMON THE SWEET SISTERS FROM THE NORTH, THE SOUTH, THE EAST AND THE WEST TO HEAR MY REQUEST AND TO PRESENT THEMSELVES HERE AT THIS TIME, THIS PLACE AND AT THIS CEREMONY TO WITNESS MY ACTIONS OF GOOD WILL SO THAT MY OFFFERINGS BRING GOOD AND LIGHT. I CALL UPON THE AJE SPIRITS, THE INVISIBLE MOTHERS OF THE NIGHT TO BE HERE BY MY SIDE. I CALL UPON THE AJE SPIRITS AND ASK THEM FOR THEIR DIVINE INTERCESSION. I HAVE NOT COME HERE TONIGHT TO FIGHT YOU OR TO CAUSE YOU HARM BECAUSE I KNOWN THAT I WILL NOT WIN AND SO THAT IS WHY I HAVE COME HERE TODAY IN PEACE AND UNIVERSAL HARMONY SO THAT YOU WILL HEAR MY REQUEST AND GRANT MY PRAYERS.

(SAY WHAT YOU WANT HERE)

STEP 3

3. After you have finished the Aje Spirits ritual you should take a spiritual bath using African Black Soap.

HOW TO WORK WITH THE AJE SPIRITS WITHOUT INITIATION

Initiation into the Congo Mysteries requires an individual to make a pact with the spiritual world. It is however possible for an individual to practice the Congo religion without going through the long process of initiations by practicing it spiritually. Although the individual who is spiritually practicing Congo religion will never fully be able to realize the benefits of an initiate who is initiated they can do this quite effectively if you approach the spirits with respect. Many individuals ask me how they can practice spiritually the Congo religion without making a pact with the powerful Congo spiritual world and the answer is very simple. An indi vidual desiring to work spiritually with the Aje spirits can do all of the following to start working with the Congo spirits.

1. *Construct a spiritual altar to the Aje Spirits.*

2. *Construct a spiritual altar to the Eggun Spirits (Ancestors).*

3. *Construct a spiritual altar called a "Boveda Espiritual".*

On your altars you can place images, statues of the Three Graces and any of the spirit signature signs that correspond to them. Candles are very important and are also key spiritual elements as part of your spiritual Aje spirit altar. When you will be invoking the Aje spirits you can simply draw the Aje spirit signature on a piece of paper and then place the candle on top of it before you invoke them through sim ple prayers in English or traditional Congo language. You can use any of the Aje Spirit prayers in this book to realize your spiritual practice of Congo Spirit worship.

HOW TO USE THIS SPELL & RITUAL BOOK

ALL OF THE FOLLOWING SPELLS & RITUALS IN THIS BOOK CAN BE DONE BY USING THE FOLLOWING RITUAL INSTRUCTIONS:

1. DETERMINE WHICH SPIRITUAL WORK IS APPROPRIATE FOR YOUR DESIRES.

2. GATHER ALL OF THE NECESSARY MAGICAL INGREDIENTS TOGETHER.

3. DETERMINE THE APPROPRIATE DAY AND THE TIME OF PERFORMING THE SACRED RITUAL.

4. PLACE THE MAGICAL WORK ON YOUR SPIRITUAL SHRINE, SPIRITUAL ALTAR.

5. SAY THE INVOCATION TO THE AJE SPIRITS.

6. BEGIN YOUR SACRED RITUAL AFTER INVOKING THE POWERS OF THE AJE SPIRITS.

7. MEDITATE ON YOUR DESIRES.

8. REPEAT THE SACRED RITUAL AS OFTEN AS YOU FEEL IS NEEDED TO ACHIEVE YOUR DESIRES.

IF IS RECCOMENDED THAT WHILE DOING ANY RITUAL FOR THE AJE SPIRITS THAT YOU RING A BRASS BELL THAT YOU SHOULD ALWAYS HAVE ON THEIR SACRED ALTAR.

AJE SPIRIT PROTECTION OIL

Very potent, protects from evil spirits and overcomes hexes.

Lavender oil

Sandalwood oil

Holy Water

Spring Water

AJE SPIRITS ANGELIC OIL

An anointing oil for Angelic Intervention or use during prayer.

Sandalwood oil

Magnolia oil

Myrrh oil

AJE SPIRIT POWER OIL

To invoke the powers of the Aje Spirits.

Almond oil

Sage oil

Dragons blood oil

1 Small crushed Garnet

AJE SPIRIT FAST LUCK OIL

Helps you find opportunity and resources.

Clove oil

Patchouli oil

Frankincense oil

Pine oil

Bergamot oil

AJE SPIRIT PROTECTION OIL

This blend is for protection against physical, mental, and emotional attacks.

Patchouli oil

Sandalwood oil

Lilac oil

AJE SPIRIT PROSPERITY OIL

For prosperity.

Cherry oil

Anise oil

Musk oil

Vanilla oil

Civet oil

AJE SPIRIT ENCHANTMENT OIL

To entice an individual for love and romance.

Rose oil

Thyme oil

Primrose oil

AJE SPIRIT LUST OIL

To bring about lust in other individuals.

Peach oil

Musk oil

Chamomile oil

Poppy oil

Ylang-Ylang oil

Dragon's blood oil

AJE SPIRIT SEDUCTION OIL

To seduce individuals around you.

1 Garnet, crushed

Dragon's blood oil

Coriander seeds

AJE SPIRIT GAMBLING LUCK OIL

To attract love and romance.

Lavender oil

Lilac oil

Jasmine oil

Rose Geranium oil

Carnation oil

Rosemary oil

AJE SPIRIT HEALTH OIL

Use this recipe to speed recovery from illness.

Carnation oil

Sandalwood oil

Rose oil

AJE SPIRIT BETWITCHING OIL

Lavender oil

Cypress oil

Apple oil

Dragon's blood oil

Hawthorn berry

Carnation oil

Gardenia oil

AJE SPIRIT LOVE & ATTRACTION OIL

To attract men.

Jasmine oil

Rose oil

Ylang Ylang oil

Gardenia oil

Violet oil

Musk oil

Lavender oil

AJE SPIRIT LUST & DESIRE OIL

Wear the oil to bewitch the one that you desire.

Lemon oil

Lavender oil

Primrose oil

Rose Geranium oil

Camphor oil

Lotus oil

China Musk oil

Rose oil

Honeysuckle oil

1 small Sea Shell, if desired to place in the bottle with the oil.

AJE SPIRIT COME TO ME OIL

Rose oil

Carnation oil

Violet oil

Sandalwood oil

CANDLE COLORS AND THEIR MAGICAL MEANINGS

Candles can be fix/dressed with any of the occult oils that were just listed in the previous chapter and burned in magical invocations to seek love, wealth, health, fortune, exorcise evil and cast spells. If you want to see good results with your magical spells then use the following candle color combinations and following their magical meanings. All of the following candle color combinations can be used with the Aje Spirits depending upon the desired magical intent of your spell. If you are unable to find these magical colored combination candles then you can use the following general colors for your spiritual work. A red candle is used to generally represent the Quimbanda Spirit, Exu Maioral, a black candle is generally used to represent the Quimbanda Spirit, Exu Rei and a White candle is generally used to represent the Quimbanda Spirit, Pomba Gira. Fixing or Dressing a candle simply means rubbing the appropriate colored candle with a corresponding magical oil.

BLACK

Used in hexing and cursing spells and rituals. Black candles can also be used to unhex and to banish away negativity.

RED

Passion, energy, power, strength, courage, achievement, magnetism, counteract fatigue and anger.

ORANGE

Attraction, motivation, mental energy, clear thinking, harmony, expansion, happiness.

WHITE

Protection, meditation, blessing, purity, health, and spiritual growth.

GRAY

Neutralizing, stops stress, masking, veiling, and hesitation.

LAVENDER

Spiritual development, psychic growth, divination, blessings, sensitivity.

PINK

Emotional love, romances, and new loves, come to me, friendship.

GOLD

Solar energy, power, physical strength, success, achievement, mental growth.

WHITE & GREEN

Protection of money, i.e. protecting one's investment.

WHITE & PINK

Protecting the harmony and love of a relationship.

WHITE & BLACK

Jinx removing, removing nasty vibes.

WHITE & PURPLE

Excellent meditation candle.

WHITE & BLUE

Protection and peace in home.

WHITE & YELLOW

Cleansing of your aura.

WHITE & ORANGE

Blessing and harmony in the home.

WHITE & RED

Protects your health.

WHITE & BROWN

Protection of children and your pets.

GREEN & BROWN

Attracting good job, proper home.

GREEN & BLUE

Prosperity.

GREEN & PURPLE

Attracting large amounts of money.

GREEN & BLACK

Banishing poverty or money problems.

RED & BROWN

Favor in legal matters.

RED & BLACK

Reversing negativity or evil to sender.

RED & PURPLE

Conquering difficult situations.

RED & GREEN

Powerful money boost for raises and promotions.

BLUE & PURPLE

Prophetic dreams.

BLUE & BLACK

Removing depression.

YELLOW & RED

Attracting love.

YELLOW & GREEN

Attracting success and money.

YELLOW & BLUE

Achieving balance.

YELLOW & BROWN

Renting or selling of a home, success.

YELLOW & BLACK

Banishing bad luck, removing blocks in your success.

YELLOW & PURPLE

Promotions, new endeavors.

YELLOW & ORANGE

Attracting success, fast luck.

ORANGE & RED

Attracting a perfect mate, solar energy.

ORANGE & YELLOW

Attracting success in the arts, music.

ORANGE & GREEN

Balance and expansion, fast luck.

ORANGE & PURPLE

Aids in studying, also power and strength.

ORANGE & BROWN

Attracts harmony, business success.

ORANGE & BLUE

Happiness, harmony, peace and clarity.

ORANGE & BLACK

Removing blocks in business success.

PINK & GREEN

Attracting a mate with money.

PINK & RED

Romance and lust in a relationship.

PINK & PURPLE

For "Come To Me Spells."

PINK & BLUE

Peace and harmony.

PINK & BROWN

Happiness and stability.

WHITE/RED/BROWN

When bad thing happen to good people.When you are not at fault, court, custody, licensing, IRS, etc.

WHITE/RED/PURPLE

When you are at fault, when you need help in overcoming a situation.

WHITE/RED/GREEN

When creditors are a bother, when wishing to attract wages to reassess how to financially proceed without interference.

WHITE/RED/BLUE

Protect my home and/or my love from all interference.

WHITE/RED/BLACK

For troubles such as magnitude, you need to dispose of quickly, so your thoughts are clear. To divine a solution burn in a waning moon for protection against interference.

WHITE/LAVANDER/BLUE

Any time you have truly lost direction, when all you have worked for has gone astray because of loss of faith in yourself and your higher power re-establishes your faith.

WHITE/GRAY/BLACK

For court cases when you are guilty, no evidence against you will be found, charges will be dropped. A sacrifice goes with this; make your sacrifice beforehand, whether it is your time, physical or monetary to those who need help.

YELLOW/GREEN/BROWN

For perfect job, attract it, get the money you want and now keep it.

YELLOW/GREEN/PURPLE

When asking for job promotion or raise, also used to increase your $$$. Note: Must have some $$$ first to do this.

YELLOW/PINK/RED

Communication with someone who's friendly to you but you would like more, a stronger bond of interaction.

YELLOW/ORANGE/RED

To attract to you the most important mate that you can have this lifetime. It is essential that you specify all situations that will be compatible with your needs.

PINK/LAVANDER/RED

When your love life has reached an impasse. To re-establish the romance and communication between both of you and the passion that may have been forgotten.

PINK/RED/PURPLE

Re-establish by attracting them back with thoughts of lust and sexual desire. Also brings someone to you with the intent of deeper passion and a sexual relationship.

PINK/BLUE/BROWN

Burn when it is necessary to have Peace, Love and Harmony in the home, especially when adult children are involved.

ORANGE/RED/PURPLE

Mandatory when breaking through those difficult situations.Especially those that involve special favor with authorities, maybe government agencies or legal problems.

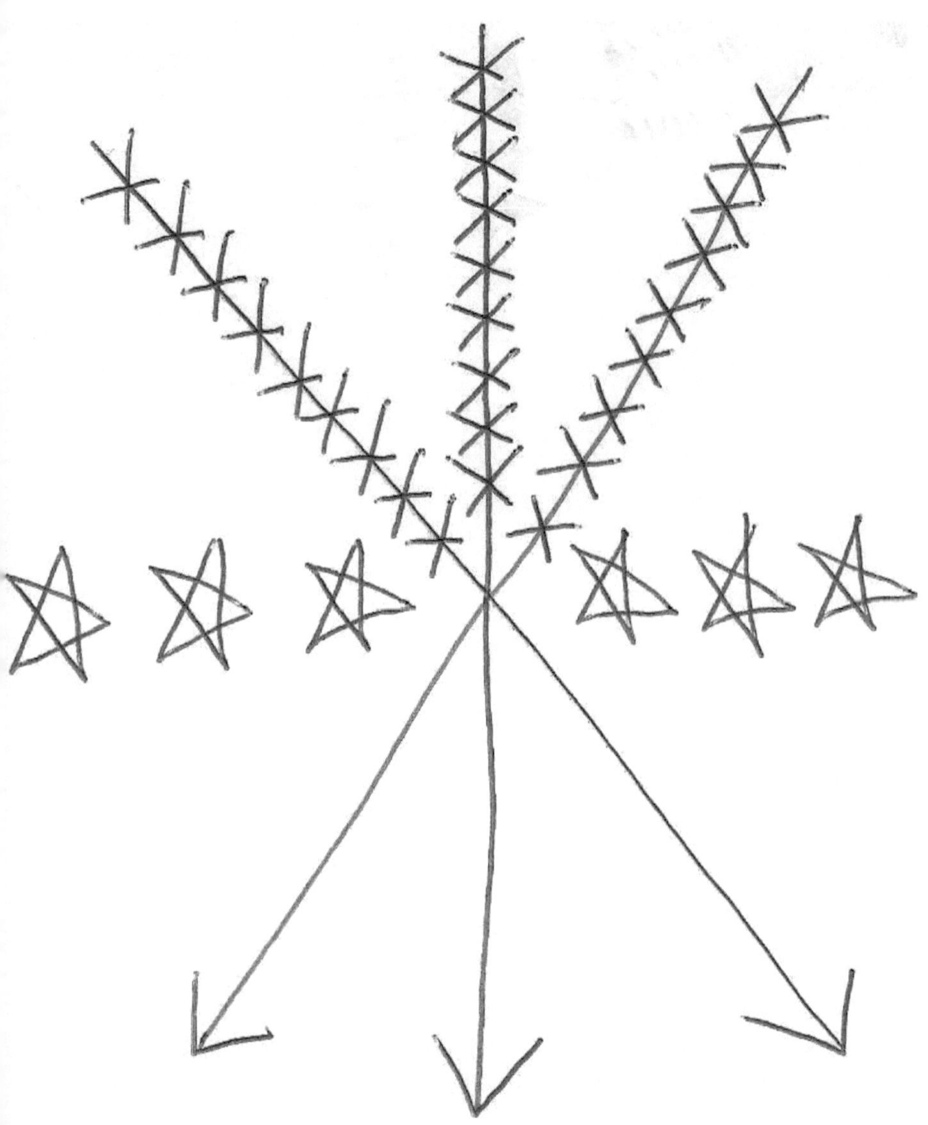

A PICTURE OF THE SACRED MAGICAL SPIRIT SYMBOL WHICH REPRESENTS THE AJE SPIRITS.

PAPA MONTENEGRO'S OCCULT SHOP would like to invite you to browse through our store and shop with confidence.

Authentic Handmade Occult Products, Quimbanda Ritual Products, Herbal Baths, Colognes, Incense, Oils, Spell Kits, Candles, Books & Sacred Art. All of our occult products are handmade.

WE CARRY OVER 1800 AUTHENTIC HANDMADE & RITUALLY PREPARED OCCULT OILS IN STOCK AT OUR STORE, MADE WITH REAL MAGICAL HERBS, ESSENTIAL OILS, FRAGRANCED OILS & RARE OCCULT SACRED INGREDIENTS.

WWW.PAPAMONTENEGRO.COM

www.ingramcontent.com/pod-product-compliance
Ingram Content Group UK Ltd.
Pitfield, Milton Keynes, MK11 3LW, UK
UKHW041924190726
13854UKWH00003B/1429